Flore

Emily Rasmus

All rights reserved. No part of this publication may be reproduced, distributed, or transmitted in any form or by any means, including photocopying, recording, or other electronic or mechanical methods, without the prior written permission of the publisher, except in the case of brief quotations embodied in critical reviews and certain other noncommercial uses permitted by copyright law.

Copyright © (Emily Rasmus) (2023).

INTRODUCTION	**7**
CHAPTER ONE	**9**
Introduction	9
• Brief History of Florence	9
• Getting Around	11
CHAPTER TWO	**17**
Essential Information	17
•Weather and Best Time to Visit	17
• Currency and Language	20
•Local Etiquette and Customs	24
CHAPTER THREE	**29**
Top Attractions	29
• The Duomo - Florence Cathedral	29
• Uffizi Gallery	32
• Ponte Vecchio	37
• Accademia Gallery and Michelangelo's David	40
• Palazzo Vecchio	44
CHAPTER FOUR	**49**
Hidden Gems	49
• Boboli Gardens	49
• San Miniato al Monte	54
• Oltrarno District	58
• The Vasari Corridor	61
CHAPTER FIVE	**65**
Culinary Delights	65

- Traditional Tuscan Cuisine — 65
- Must-Try Restaurants — 69
- Street Food Recommendations — 71

CHAPTER SIX — 77
Shopping in Florence — 77
- Florence's Markets — 77
- High-end Boutiques — 81
- Local Artisans and Crafts — 85

CHAPTER SEVEN — 89
Day Trips from Florence — 89
- Siena — 89
- Pisa — 93
- Chianti Region — 96
- Cinque Terre — 100

CHAPTER EIGHT — 105
Cultural Experiences — 105
- Opera and Classical Performances — 105
- Festivals and Events — 109
- Florence's Art Scene — 112

CHAPTER NINE — 117
Practical Tips — 117
- Transportation Tips — 117
- Safety and Health — 120
- Local Customs to Be Aware Of — 123

CHAPTER TEN — 127
Itinerary Suggestions — 127
- One Day in Florence — 127
- Weekend Getaway — 130

CHAPTER ELEVEN — 133

Conclusion	133
• Final Thoughts	133

INTRODUCTION

Welcome to Florence, a fascinating cultural tapestry where art and history collide. As you travel through this charming city, get ready to be mesmerised by the Renaissance charm that adorns each cobblestone street and famous site. Florence welcomes you to discover its rich history, enjoy delicious food, and lose yourself in the enduring charm that has enthralled tourists for ages, from the majestic Uffizi Gallery to the eternal grandeur of the Duomo. Come along with me on a virtual tour of Florence, where hidden stories await discovery around every turn.

CHAPTER ONE

Introduction

• Brief History of Florence

Florence, known as the "Cradle of the Renaissance," is a city in central Tuscany with a rich history that has influenced the city's identity in terms of culture, art, and architecture.

When Florence was founded in the first century BCE as a community for retired Roman soldiers, the city's history officially began. It developed over the ages into a prosperous mediaeval city-state and a centre of banking and trade.

The Renaissance, which lasted from the 14th to the 17th century, brought forth Florence's golden period. An important factor in the city's cultural rebirth was the Medici family, prominent benefactors of the humanities and sciences. The streets and museums of Florence bear the permanent imprint of the inspiration and assistance that artists such as Michelangelo, Botticelli, and Leonardo da Vinci received here.

Florence's architectural prowess is demonstrated by the Duomo, the city's landmark church with its beautiful dome created by Brunelleschi. Once serving as the Medici family's headquarters, the Uffizi Gallery is now home to an acclaimed collection of Renaissance masterpieces.

But political upheavals have also occurred in Florence's past. The Medici dynasty was beset by events such as the legendary Bonfire of the Vanities in 1497, which saw religious fanatics destroy literature and artwork they deemed to be immoral. Later, Florence was ruled by the Habsburgs and then the House of Lorraine, as part of the Grand Duchy of Tuscany.

Florence was chosen to serve as the capital of the newly united Italy in the 19th century. The city accepted industrialization while keeping its creative legacy intact. The magnificent Ponte Vecchio, a mediaeval bridge spanning the Arno River, has withstood World War II and has come to represent the fortitude of Florence.

Every palazzo and cobblestone street in Florence still acts as a living museum, whispering stories about its illustrious past.

Explore the former Medici house, Pitti Palace, and take a leisurely stroll around the Boboli Gardens, which offer sweeping views of the city. The timeless masterpiece David by Michelangelo is kept at the Accademia Gallery.

The history of Florence comes to life as you stroll through its streets. Every area has a story to tell, from Oltrarno's artisan crafts to Piazza della Signoria's mediaeval splendour. With its rich history, the city's food scene provides a taste of genuine Tuscan flavours that have developed over generations.

Florence is essentially a mesmerising fusion of the old and the new, a place where the aura of the Renaissance clings, beckoning visitors to experience both the lively energy of contemporary Italy and a trip back in time.

- **Getting Around**

It's a lovely trip through history, art, and culture to navigate Florence. I can't help but be enthralled by this city's ageless beauty and the way that Renaissance charm and contemporary conveniences mesh so perfectly as I explore it. I'll share my travel experiences and advice on getting around Florence in this travel guide to help you make the most of your trip.

Investigating on Foot

The city of Florence is one that should be explored gradually. As you stroll down its cobblestone lanes, you'll come across famous sites at every bend. The pedestrian-friendly and tiny old centre is perfect for touring on foot, and it is recognised as a UNESCO World Heritage site. Wandering through the centre of the city, Piazza della Signoria, I am surrounded by magnificent sculptures and the massive Palazzo Vecchio.

Wear Comfy Shoes
Wear comfy footwear. Wearing comfortable shoes is crucial, as you will be exploring stunning bridges, winding through little lanes, and passing through large squares.

Viewing the City
To improve your walking experience, become familiar with the locations of the important sites. Visible from several angles, the Duomo, or Florence Cathedral, acts as a primary point of reference.

Using Public Transit

Even though the historic centre is a pedestrian's paradise, there are times when taking public transport is essential, particularly if you're visiting the surrounding areas or your feet need a break.

Florence Bus System
Different neighbourhoods are effectively connected by the ATAF bus system. Tickets can be purchased on the bus itself or at kiosks. Buses are a practical means of transportation to places like Fiesole, a nearby hill village with stunning views of Florence.

Florence Tramway
Another dependable form of transportation is the tramway. It establishes a link between the city centre and its environs. To ensure that your trip is well-planned, review the tram routes.

Cycling in Florence

Bicycling is a well-liked and environmentally responsible way to see Florence, embracing the local way of life. All skill levels of cyclists may enter the city thanks to its bike-friendly infrastructure and generally level terrain.

Rent a Bike
From traditional bicycles toelectric bikes, there are several places to rent bikes. Riding a bike through Cascine Park or alongside the Arno River offers a revitalising viewpoint of the city.

Cycle Lanes
Use the bike lanes that are allocated for you. Cycling has been encouraged in Florence in a big way, with designated routes making for a fun and safe ride across the city.

Ride-sharing and Taxis

In Florence, it's easy to find taxis and ride-sharing services for a more private and convenient travel alternative.

Stands for Taxis
In well-travelled locations, look for authorised taxi stands or hail a cab. Make sure the taxi's metre is operating, and it's a good idea to have cash on hand to pay the fare.

Anchorage-Sharing Apps
Traditional taxis can be replaced by local alternatives or apps like Uber. They provide cashless payment and ride tracking, which is convenient.

The Emblematic Florence Ape

A distinctive way to travel that gives your trip a dash of Italian style is the famous Ape, a three-wheeled car that is frequently transformed into a tiny taxi or roving seller.

Go Ape

A unique way to see the city is to go on an APE tour. These little cars can fit through the tiny streets and offer a more individualised and intimate tour experience.

Arno Boat Rides

The Arno River, which meanders through Florence, offers the opportunity to see the city from a fresh angle—by boat.

Arno River Tours:

Numerous businesses provide boat cruises with guides along the Arno. These tours give a distinctive viewpoint and frequently include commentary on the historical sites that line the riverbanks.

Finding Your Way Around Museums and Attractions

World-class museums and art galleries may be found throughout Florence, adding to the city's rich cultural heritage. Getting around these jewels takes considerable preparation.

Reservations for Museums

Purchase your tickets in advance, particularly for well-known sites like the Accademia and Uffizi Galleries. By doing this, you not only avoid missing out on these cultural treasures but also save time.

Municipal Passes
If you want access to a variety of attractions, think about getting a city pass. These passes frequently come with the ability to skip the queue, which will improve the efficiency of your museum-hopping experience.

CHAPTER TWO

Essential Information

•Weather and Best Time to Visit

A visit to Florence, the charming city tucked away in the centre of Tuscany, is made even more fascinating by its varied climate. Knowing Florence's weather trends in advance will make your trip much more enjoyable. Let me help you decide when is the best time to visit this hidden jewel of Italy as an experienced traveller who has explored the cobblestone lanes and historical sites.

Springtime Glimmer: March through May

Going on a springtime excursion in Florence is like walking upon a live painting. Every area of the city is covered in blossoms, causing it to explode in colour. The weather, which is between 10 and 20 degrees Celsius (50 and 68 degrees Fahrenheit), provides a comfortable setting for exploring the famous Piazza della Signoria or scaling the Duomo.

The pavements are overrun with cafés, and the soft breeze fills the air with the lovely aroma of budding flowers. Take advantage of this time to visit the Boboli Gardens, where sculptures and colourful vegetation combine to create a peaceful haven. Florence's springtime captures the spirit of rebirth, making it the perfect season for both nature and art lovers.

Charms of Summer: June to August

Summer embraces Florence warmly as the sun rises higher in the Tuscan sky. The city becomes a vibrant refuge as the temperatures soar to an average of 30 degrees Celsius (86°F). You have plenty of time to fully immerse yourself in Florence's rich cultural diversity, thanks to the longer daylight hours.

The city is alive with energy thanks to street performances, outdoor concerts, and art festivals. But be ready for more crowds, particularly in the vicinity of well-known sites like Ponte Vecchio and the Uffizi Gallery. If you want to avoid the midday sun, you might want to take a relaxing afternoon nap before continuing to discover Florence's wonders.

Artistry of Autumn: September through November

Autumn is when Florence shows off another fascinating side as summer comes to an end. September retains much of the summer's warmth before progressively cooling off in October and November. The city's ageless beauty is enhanced by the crisp air, which gives it a golden glow.

Autumn is the best season to enjoy regional food at alfresco trattorias and take in the changing foliage. The city's artistic and historical richness can be experienced without the summertime throngs, thanks to the lively cultural calendar that is still in place. Remember to stroll through Oltrarno's winding lanes, where artisan workshops entice you with their genuine Florentine craftsmanship.

Winter Temptations: December through February

A calm atmosphere permeates Florence as winter closes in. Even though it can be as cold as 3°C (37°F), there aren't many people around to create a cosy environment that makes it peaceful to visit famous sites like the Florence Cathedral and Palazzo Pitti.

Winter also means the return of lively markets, where the sounds of street performers blend with the aroma of roast chestnuts. When it drizzles, the Uffizi Gallery and other interior sites turn into comfortable havens. For those who prefer a more introspective and alone experience, winter may be the perfect season to explore Florence's past at their own leisure.

• Currency and Language

Situated in the centre of Tuscany, Florence enthrals tourists with its abundant artistic, historical, and cultural legacy. As I strolled through its cobblestone streets, I couldn't help but notice the seamless fusion of two vital elements that define any society – currency and language.

The local currency in Florence, as in the rest of Italy, is the Euro. The Euro became the official currency in 2002, replacing the Italian Lira. As I exchanged my currency at a local bank, I marveled at the intricate designs on the Euro bills, each telling a story of Europe's history and cultural diversity. In Florence, the Euro served not only as a medium of exchange but also as a symbol of the city's integration into the broader European community.

Language, too, played a pivotal role in my Florentine experience. Italian, the official language of the country, echoed through the narrow streets, cafes, and historic sites. Engaging with locals in their native tongue added a layer of authenticity to my journey, enabling me to connect on a deeper level. From ordering a cappuccino at a quaint coffee shop to navigating the renowned Uffizi Gallery, speaking Italian enriched my exploration of Florence.

Moreover, the Florentine dialect, a variant of Tuscan Italian, added a distinctive local flavor to conversations. While many residents are fluent in standard Italian, hearing the melodic cadence of the Florentine dialect was a reminder of the city's unique identity. It highlighted the significance of language as a cultural bridge, allowing me to immerse myself in the traditions and nuances of Florence.

The influence of language and currency converged seamlessly in the bustling markets of Florence. As I haggled over the price of leather goods at the San Lorenzo Market, the negotiation dance was accompanied by the rhythm of Italian words and the exchange of

Euros. The market, a vibrant tapestry of colors and sounds, served as a microcosm of Florence's cultural and economic exchanges.

Delving deeper into Florence's history, I discovered the impact of currency on the city's artistic legacy. The florin, a gold coin minted in Florence from the 13th to the 17th century, played a crucial role in the flourishing of the Renaissance. The Medici family, prominent patrons of the arts, used the florin to commission masterpieces from renowned artists like Leonardo da Vinci and Michelangelo. The remnants of this artistic patronage are scattered throughout Florence, from the magnificent sculptures in the Piazza della Signoria to the intricate frescoes in the Medici Chapels.

Language, on the other hand, was the brushstroke that painted the literary landscape of Florence. The works of Dante Alighieri, Petrarch, and Boccaccio, written in the Tuscan dialect, laid the foundation for modern Italian. Standing before the statue of Dante in the Piazza Santa Croce, I couldn't help but appreciate the profound impact of language on shaping the city's cultural and intellectual legacy.

In the contemporary context, Florence continues to be a hub of art, commerce, and cultural exchange. The city's language schools attract students from around the globe, eager to learn Italian in the very heart of its origin. These linguistic endeavors contribute to the cosmopolitan atmosphere of Florence, where diverse voices intertwine with the echoes of the past.

As I navigated the corridors of the Uffizi Gallery, home to an unparalleled collection of Renaissance art, I observed the multilingual nature of the visitors. English, Spanish, Chinese – a symphony of languages reverberated through the halls, underscoring Florence's role as a global cultural destination. The multilingualism embraced by the city reflects its openness to a myriad of perspectives and narratives.

Furthermore, Florence's commitment to preserving its linguistic and cultural heritage is evident in the efforts to protect the Florentine dialect. Local initiatives promote the use of the dialect in everyday conversation and celebrate its unique linguistic features. This dedication to linguistic diversity reinforces Florence's identity as a city that values its roots while embracing the global community.

•Local Etiquette and Customs

Exploring Florence introduces you to a rich tapestry of local etiquette and customs, woven into the very fabric of this enchanting city. As a seasoned traveler, embracing these cultural nuances enhances your experience and fosters meaningful connections with the locals.

Greeting Rituals:
Upon arriving in Florence, you'll quickly notice the significance placed on greetings. A warm "Buongiorno" (good morning) sets the tone for interactions. Handshakes are common, but don't be surprised by the warmth of cheek-kissing among friends and even acquaintances. It's a gesture deeply embedded in Italian culture, symbolizing familiarity and friendship.

Dining Etiquette:
Dining in Florence is a celebration of flavors and camaraderie. Respect for food is paramount, and meals are savored slowly, allowing time for conversation. It's customary to wait for the host or hostess to initiate the

first bite. If you find yourself invited to a local home, a small gift as a token of appreciation is a thoughtful gesture.

Café Culture:
The city's vibrant café culture is a quintessential part of daily life. Take a cue from the locals and savor your espresso standing at the bar, immersing yourself in the lively atmosphere. Remember, tipping is not as customary in Italy as it is in some other countries. While appreciated, it's not obligatory, as service charges are often included in the bill.

Respecting Art and Architecture:
Florence is a living museum, boasting some of the world's most revered art and architecture. When visiting churches and museums, modest attire is a sign of respect. Shoulders and knees should be covered, especially when entering sacred spaces. Conversing in hushed tones reinforces the reverence for the art that surrounds you.

Navigating Public Spaces:
Stroll through Florence, and you'll find the city teeming with life. When navigating crowded streets, a polite "scusi" (excuse me) goes a long

way. The pace of life here is leisurely, so there's no need to rush. Embrace the art of the "passeggiata," an evening stroll taken for the sheer pleasure of it.

market Etiquette:
The bustling markets of Florence, like Mercato Centrale, offer a sensory explosion. Engage with vendors respectfully, and don't hesitate to haggle a bit—it's part of the experience. Remember to handle produce with care, appreciating the freshness that defines Tuscan cuisine.

Language Appreciation:
While many Florentians speak English, making an effort to speak Italian is genuinely appreciated. Basic phrases like "grazie" (thank you) and "prego" (you're welcome) showcase your respect for the local language and culture.

Festivals and Celebrations:
Florence comes alive during festivals like Easter, Calcio Storico, and the Festa della Rificolona. Participate with a spirit of enthusiasm, embracing the local customs and revelry. Whether watching the historical football match or enjoying the lantern parade,

these events provide a unique glimpse into the city's traditions.

Tipping and Payment:
While tipping is not obligatory, rounding up the bill or leaving a few extra euros is a courteous gesture, especially if the service has been exceptional. Credit cards are widely accepted, but it's advisable to carry some cash for smaller establishments.

Adapting to Siesta Time:
Florence, like much of Italy, observes a siesta period in the afternoon when many shops close for a few hours. Embrace this rhythm, perhaps indulging in a leisurely lunch or a quiet stroll along the Arno River.

CHAPTER THREE

Top Attractions

• The Duomo - Florence Cathedral

The Duomo, also known as the Florence Cathedral, stands as a majestic masterpiece in the heart of Florence, Italy. As I embarked on my journey through this enchanting city, the Duomo captivated my senses and became an undeniable highlight of my Florence experience. Its rich history, stunning architecture, and cultural significance make it a must-visit attraction that defines the essence of Florence.

Ascending towards the Duomo, the grandeur of its exterior is impossible to ignore. The cathedral's intricate facade, adorned with marble panels and sculptures, narrates tales of religious devotion and artistic brilliance. Gazing upon it, one can't help but marvel at the craftsmanship that went into creating this architectural marvel, reflecting the artistic prowess of the Renaissance era.

The centerpiece of the Duomo complex is the iconic dome designed by Filippo Brunelleschi. As I ventured inside, the sheer magnitude of the dome's interior left me in awe. The frescoes that decorate the dome, including Giorgio Vasari's Last Judgment, transport visitors into a world where art and spirituality converge seamlessly. Climbing to the top of the dome offered panoramic views of Florence, rewarding my ascent with a breathtaking vista that made every step worthwhile.

Adjacent to the cathedral is the Campanile, Giotto's bell tower, another gem in Florence's architectural crown. Its ornate design and captivating sculptures make it a testament to the city's commitment to artistic excellence. Climbing the tower provided a unique perspective on the cityscape, offering a different angle of Florence's beauty.

The Baptistery, dedicated to St. John the Baptist, completes the Duomo complex. Its renowned bronze doors, including Lorenzo Ghiberti's Gates of Paradise, stand as masterpieces of Renaissance art. Stepping inside, the elegant interior and the renowned mosaic ceiling transported me to a bygone era, leaving an indelible impression of Florence's rich cultural heritage.

Beyond its architectural grandeur, the Duomo holds immense religious significance. As the seat of the Archbishop of Florence, it plays a central role in the religious life of the city. Witnessing a religious service within its hallowed halls provided a glimpse into the spiritual heartbeat of Florence, connecting the past with the present in a profound way.

The Piazza del Duomo, the square surrounding the cathedral, buzzes with life. Street performers, artisans, and vibrant cafes create an atmosphere that is quintessentially Italian. It's a place to soak in the energy of Florence, surrounded by centuries of history and culture.

The Duomo's influence extends beyond its physical presence; it permeates the cultural fabric of Florence. Museums and galleries throughout the city showcase religious artifacts and artworks inspired by the cathedral. The impact of the Duomo on Florence's identity is undeniable, making it a focal point for both locals and visitors alike.

Exploring the Duomo is not just a visual experience; it's an auditory and sensory journey. The echo of footsteps in the cathedral's nave, the whispers of prayers, and the occasional notes of sacred music create a symphony that resonates through time. It's a profound encounter with the spiritual and artistic soul of Florence.

The ongoing preservation efforts of the Duomo highlight the city's commitment to safeguarding its cultural heritage. Restoration projects ensure that future generations can continue to marvel at this architectural wonder, fostering a sense of continuity and shared legacy.

- **Uffizi Gallery**

The Uffizi Gallery, a renowned art museum in Florence, stands as a cultural jewel and a must-visit destination for art enthusiasts. Nestled in the heart of the city, this iconic attraction offers a captivating journey through the world of Italian Renaissance art. As I embarked on my Florence adventure, the Uffizi Gallery beckoned with promises of timeless masterpieces and a glimpse into the artistic legacy of this enchanting city.

Upon entering the gallery, I was immediately struck by the grandeur of the architecture, a testament to the rich history that unfolded within its walls. Originally designed by Giorgio Vasari in the 16th century to house government offices ("uffizi" in Italian), the building's transformation into an art repository has solidified its place in history. Its location, adjacent to the Piazza della Signoria and overlooking the Arno River, adds to the allure, making it a central hub for cultural exploration.

The Uffizi Gallery boasts an extensive collection of over 2,000 works of art, showcasing the evolution of Italian art from the Middle Ages to the Renaissance and beyond. As I strolled through the labyrinthine corridors, I found myself face to face with masterpieces by artists whose names resonate through the ages – Giotto, Botticelli, Leonardo da Vinci, Michelangelo, Raphael, and Caravaggio, among others. Each brushstroke and sculpted form told a story, inviting me to unravel the mysteries of creativity that defined these eras.

One of the highlights of the Uffizi experience is encountering Sandro Botticelli's "The Birth of Venus" and "Primavera." These iconic works, bathed in ethereal beauty, encapsulate the essence of the Renaissance period. The delicate grace of Venus emerging from the sea and the allegorical richness of "Primavera" left an indelible imprint on my artistic sensibilities. Witnessing these paintings in person was like stepping into a time capsule, where myth and reality converged in a visual symphony.

The Uffizi Gallery's layout is organized chronologically, allowing visitors to traverse the artistic evolution of Florence and Italy. From early religious paintings to the groundbreaking innovations of the Renaissance, the gallery acts as a visual timeline, offering a comprehensive education in art history. I found myself marveling at the transition from the Byzantine style to the revolutionary techniques of perspective and chiaroscuro that defined the Renaissance.

One cannot discuss the Uffizi Gallery without mentioning Leonardo da Vinci's "Annunciation." The master's meticulous attention to detail and his pioneering use of light and shadow are on full display in this masterpiece. As I gazed at the ethereal scene, I couldn't help but appreciate the genius that laid the groundwork for centuries of artistic exploration.

The Uffizi is not merely a repository of paintings; its sculpture collection adds another layer to the narrative of artistic achievement. Works like Michelangelo's "Tondo Doni" and Giambologna's "Rape of the Sabine Women" showcase the mastery of form and emotion that defined the sculptural contributions of the Renaissance.

As I meandered through the various rooms, I encountered the haunting beauty of Caravaggio's "Medusa" and the timeless elegance of Raphael's "Madonna of the Goldfinch." The diverse range of styles and subjects ensured that every turn brought a new visual feast, leaving me in awe of the artistic richness curated within these walls.

The Uffizi Gallery is not solely a repository of historical artifacts; it is a living testament to the cultural identity of Florence. The Vasari Corridor, a secret passageway connecting the Uffizi to the Pitti Palace, allows visitors to walk in the footsteps of the powerful Medici family, who commissioned many of the artworks on display. This clandestine route, usually closed to the public, provides a unique perspective on the city and its artistic heritage.

A visit to the Uffizi Gallery is a sensory journey, and the rooftop terrace offers a moment of respite amidst the artistic splendor. Overlooking the city, the terrace provides a panoramic view of Florence, allowing visitors to appreciate the interconnectedness of art and landscape. The red-tiled roofs, the Arno River winding through the city, and the distant hills create a picturesque backdrop that complements the visual feast within the gallery.

Navigating the Uffizi Gallery can be an overwhelming experience, given the sheer volume of artworks on display. To enhance my visit, I opted for an audio guide, which provided insightful commentary on key pieces. This added layer of information deepened my understanding of the artistic techniques, historical contexts, and the personal stories behind each masterpiece.

To fully immerse oneself in the Uffizi experience, it's advisable to plan the visit strategically. Booking tickets in advance and visiting during off-peak hours can help avoid long queues, ensuring more time to savor the art. Additionally, taking breaks in the museum's café or courtyard allows for reflection and rejuvenation amid the visual banquet.

The Uffizi Gallery is not merely a top attraction in Florence; it is a pilgrimage for art lovers and a gateway to the soul of Italian Renaissance art. Its curated collection serves as a visual encyclopedia, narrating the story of Florence's cultural evolution. As I bid farewell to the Uffizi, I carried with me not only memories of breathtaking art but also a profound appreciation for the indelible mark that Florence has left on the world's artistic legacy.

- **Ponte Vecchio**

A timeless treasure tucked away in Florence's centre, Ponte Vecchio is a compelling reminder of the city's magnificent architecture and rich past. When I started my tour of Florence, this famous bridge stood out as a must-see since it combined art, history, and breath-taking Arno River views.

The Arno River is crossed by the pedestrian Ponte Vecchio, sometimes known as the "Old Bridge" in English. Its origins are in the Middle Ages; the first bridge was destroyed by flooding, and the current structure was completed in 1345. I was taken to a bygone period as I strolled along its storied arches, where the sounds of craftsmen and merchants seemed to linger in the air.

The distinctive stores that flank both sides of Ponte Vecchio are among its most alluring features. Since the Renaissance, the "botteghe," or shops, have been a defining feature of the bridge. The stores are currently home to a variety of jewellers, art dealers, and souvenir shops, having once been occupied by butchers. The brilliant displays of jewellery made of gold and silver shimmered in the sunlight, producing an amazing kaleidoscope of artistry.

I couldn't help but notice how the bridge changed from a busy marketplace to a haven for artists and connoisseurs as I perused these charming businesses. Anyone strolling along Ponte Vecchio's cobblestone promenade is in for a sensory feast as they take in the building's blend of historic elegance and modern craftsmanship.

The Vasari Corridor, an elevated corridor that links the Palazzo Pitti to the Palazzo Vecchio, is another feature of the bridge. The Medici family commissioned this covert tunnel in 1565 so they could travel between their homes without coming into contact with the general public. There's a sense of mystery and fascination to the encounter since you can see glimpses of this tunnel as you cross the bridge now.

Ponte Vecchio not only acts as an architectural marvel but also affords unrivalled panoramic views of the Arno River and the metropolis beyond. The bridge is bathed in a warm glow during the golden hour, when the sun dips below the magnificent hills, leaving a memorable impression on those who come.

Because of its advantageous location, the bridge is a great place to start your exploration of Florence's historic district. From Ponte Vecchio, take a leisurely stroll to the Uffizi Gallery, which houses a world-class collection of Renaissance paintings. The Palazzo Pitti and the Boboli Gardens are close by, adding to Ponte Vecchio's charm and positioning it at the intersection of Florence's cultural assets.

I was in awe of the bridge's endurance as I looked upon it, seeing it endure decades of alterations and development. Ponte Vecchio's tenacity is a reflection of Florence's enduring character, which embraces the past while continuously changing to become a symbol of human achievement, art, and culture.

- **Accademia Gallery and Michelangelo's David**

The Accademia Gallery, located in the heart of Florence, stands as a testament to the city's rich artistic heritage. One cannot explore Florence without immersing oneself in the artistic marvels housed within this renowned museum. Among its many treasures, Michelangelo's David stands out as a symbol of Renaissance perfection, drawing visitors from across the globe.

As I stepped into the Accademia Gallery, I was instantly captivated by the aura of creativity that permeates its halls. The gallery showcases an extensive collection of Italian art, but it is Michelangelo's David that steals the spotlight. The sheer magnitude of this masterpiece is awe-inspiring, as it commands attention from the moment one lays eyes on it.

The journey to David begins with a stroll through rooms filled with other notable works by Michelangelo, offering a glimpse into the artist's genius. Sculptures such as the unfinished Prisoners, which seem to emerge organically from the stone, serve as a prelude to the grandeur that awaits. Each piece in the collection unveils a layer of Michelangelo's artistic evolution, providing a context that heightens the anticipation for the main event.

As I approached the hall housing David, a palpable sense of excitement enveloped me. The grandeur of the sculpture unfolded gradually, revealed by the careful arrangement of the space. Bathed in natural light streaming through strategically placed windows, David stood tall and resolute, an embodiment of human strength and beauty.

The mastery of Michelangelo's David lies not only in its imposing size but also in the meticulous attention to detail. Every sinew, every muscle, seems to pulse with life, frozen in the moment before the legendary battle with Goliath. The sculpture's expressive eyes convey a mix of determination and contemplation, inviting viewers to ponder the essence of human potential.

Beyond its artistic brilliance, David holds historical significance as a symbol of Florence's resilience and civic pride. Originally commissioned as a symbol of the city's defense of liberty, the statue became a potent emblem of the Renaissance spirit. Standing before David, one cannot escape the feeling of being in the presence of a cultural icon that transcends time.

The Accademia Gallery's commitment to preserving and showcasing Michelangelo's David is a testament to Florence's dedication to its artistic legacy. The careful conservation efforts ensure that visitors can experience the sculpture in all its glory, appreciating the nuances of Michelangelo's chisel strokes and the marble's natural textures.

Visitors to the Accademia Gallery not only witness Michelangelo's David but also gain insight into the artist's creative process. The Gipsoteca dell'Istituto d'Arte di Firenze, an integral part of the gallery, displays plaster casts of Michelangelo's works, providing a rare glimpse into the evolution of his ideas. This insightful journey enriches the overall experience, allowing art enthusiasts to connect with the artistic genius on a deeper level.

The Accademia Gallery extends beyond Michelangelo's masterpiece, presenting a comprehensive collection of Renaissance art. Works by artists such as Sandro Botticelli,

Domenico Ghirlandaio, and Filippo Lippi adorn the walls, creating a nuanced tapestry of the era's artistic achievements. Each piece contributes to the rich narrative of Florence's cultural history, offering a holistic exploration of the city's artistic heritage.

The ambiance within the Accademia Gallery is enhanced by its architecture, which seamlessly blends tradition with modernity. The expansive halls and high ceilings create a sense of grandeur, allowing visitors to immerse themselves in the artistry surrounding them. The museum's commitment to creating a conducive environment for artistic appreciation elevates the entire experience, making it a must-visit destination in Florence.

In addition to the artistic treasures, the Accademia Gallery provides educational programs and initiatives. These efforts aim to engage visitors of all ages and backgrounds, fostering a deeper understanding and appreciation of art. From guided tours to interactive workshops, the gallery's commitment to education ensures that its cultural significance continues to resonate with future generations.

A visit to the Accademia Gallery is not merely a passive encounter with art; it is a dynamic engagement with the cultural soul of Florence. The museum's role as a custodian of artistic heritage is complemented by its dedication to facilitating meaningful connections between visitors and the masterpieces on display.

Florence itself serves as a picturesque backdrop to the Accademia Gallery, enhancing the overall allure of the experience. The city's medieval streets, adorned with architectural wonders, lead visitors on a journey through time. The proximity of the gallery to other cultural landmarks, such as the Florence Cathedral and the Uffizi Gallery, makes it a pivotal stop for those seeking to unravel the layers of Florence's artistic legacy.

- **Palazzo Vecchio**

With its breathtaking architecture, cultural relevance, and abundance of art within its walls, Palazzo Vecchio is a remarkable tribute to Florence's long history. As I take you around this magical city, let's explore the reasons why Palazzo Vecchio is a must-see sight.

Revealing Florence's Golden Jewel

Located in the centre of Florence, Palazzo Vecchio is the most iconic representation of the political and cultural might of the city. With its majestic building dominating the Piazza della Signoria, it welcomes inquisitive visitors into a realm where architecture, art, and history all come together.

The History of the Palazzo

I feel as though I have travelled back in time to the early 14th century, when the Palazzo Vecchio was first built. Formerly called the Palazzo della Signoria, it housed the government of the Florentine Republic. The imposing Torre d'Arnolfo tower stands guard, resounding with stories of political intrigue and power conflicts that have taken place within these walls.

Museum of Architecture: A Visual Extravaganza

Admiring its Renaissance design, I will lead you through Palazzo Vecchio's complexities. Perforating the Florentine sky with its Medici coat of arms, the crenellated tower offers sweeping vistas of the city below. The stone facade's rustication lends a hint of mediaeval grandeur, which contrasts well with the classical components that represent the changing tastes of the era.

Beautiful Courtyard: The Outdoor Museum

The large courtyard calls to us as we investigate the inner sanctum of the Palazzo. This area becomes an outdoor museum featuring sculptures by notable artists like Giambologna's "Rape of the Sabine Women" and Cellini's magnificent bronze "Perseus with the Head of Medusa." Every monument reveals stories of creativity and mythology, giving each visitor a fully immersive experience.

The Cinquecento Salone: An Immense Masterwork

We reach the Salone dei Cinquecento after climbing the regal staircase, which is an enormous hall that astounds me. Grand Duke Cosimo I de' Medici commissioned Giorgio Vasari to paint epic murals in this enormous hall that represent important moments in Florentine history. The room's size and the artwork's astounding scope leave a lasting effect on everyone who enters.

Secrets of the Palazzo: Undiscovered Treasures and Oddities

Discovering the obscure nooks and crannies of Palazzo Vecchio takes our journey in an exciting new direction. Francesco I's studiolo, a private room with elaborate cupboards, showcases the Grand Duke's love of gathering unusual and exotic items. A sense of mystery is added by the hidden entrances and passageways, which encourage reflection on the palace's illustrious past.

The Medici Relationship: The Medici Residence in Palazzo Vecchio

In addition to being the centre of politics, Palazzo Vecchio was a testament to the might of the Medici family. I tell stories of the Medici's lavish lifestyle, their shrewd marriages, and the cultural Renaissance they fostered as we meander through their magnificent private rooms.

Museo della Città, Palazzo Vecchio as a Cultural Hub

We continue our exploration as we enter the Palazzo's Museo della Città, which is home to a sizable collection of artefacts. The museum displays Florence's cultural progression from priceless tapestries to Renaissance paintings, making it a wonderful resource for anybody wishing to gain a thorough appreciation of the city's cultural tapestry.

The Tower: An Observation of Florence from Above

Upon reaching the summit of Torre d'Arnolfo, we are greeted with an amazing view. The famous sites, such as the Florence Cathedral and Ponte Vecchio, are visible as the city's red-tiled roofs spread out below us. The immersive experience offers a distinctive viewpoint on the design of the city and its timeless beauty.

CHAPTER FOUR

Hidden Gems

• Boboli Gardens

Hidden amidst the bustling streets of Florence, the Boboli Gardens stand as an enchanting haven, largely undiscovered by the hurried footsteps of many travelers. As I strolled through this verdant masterpiece, I couldn't help but marvel at the serenity that envelops this lush oasis, hidden in plain sight.

Tucked behind the imposing Pitti Palace, the Boboli Gardens unravel a tapestry of botanical wonders and architectural marvels. One can't help but feel a sense of discovery as they venture beyond the palace's grandeur and into this green sanctuary. The air is infused with the fragrance of blooming flowers, and the symphony of chirping birds provides a delightful backdrop.

The Boboli Gardens offer a respite from the crowded attractions that define Florence. It's as if you've stumbled upon a secret garden, a tranquil retreat that contrasts sharply with the energy of the city's historic center. The paths wind through meticulously landscaped lawns, adorned with statues and fountains that seem frozen in time. Every step unveils a new facet of this hidden gem, urging visitors to savor the moments of quiet contemplation.

What makes the Boboli Gardens truly special is their historical significance. Designed in the 16th century, these gardens bear witness to centuries of art, culture, and the changing fortunes of Florence. The Medici family, renowned patrons of the Renaissance, envisioned this space as an outdoor museum, where nature and art would seamlessly blend. As I wandered through the Cypress-lined avenues, I felt a profound connection to the past, each sculpture and fountain echoing the whispers of a bygone era.

One cannot ignore the panoramic views that the Boboli Gardens generously offer. The elevated vantage points provide sweeping vistas of Florence's iconic skyline, with the red-tiled roofs of the city unfolding beneath. It's a viewpoint that not only captures the architectural prowess of Florence but also offers a moment of introspection, as if time itself is suspended.

While many travelers flock to the Uffizi Gallery or the Duomo, the Boboli Gardens remain a relatively unexplored gem. The lack of crowds fosters an intimate experience, allowing visitors to forge a personal connection with the surroundings. I found solace in the shaded groves and quiet corners, where I could escape the hustle and bustle of the more frequented attractions.

The diversity of flora in the Boboli Gardens is staggering. From ancient oaks to vibrant roses, the botanical richness mirrors the cultural tapestry of Florence. As I meandered through the Isolotto, an island adorned with sculptures and a pond, I couldn't help but appreciate the meticulous planning that went into creating this haven. Each section of the gardens felt like a chapter in a novel, contributing to the overarching narrative of Florence's artistic legacy.

The Boboli Gardens also serve as an open-air gallery, showcasing an impressive collection of sculptures from renowned artists such as Giambologna and Buontalenti. These masterpieces are thoughtfully placed, creating a harmonious dialogue with the natural surroundings. It's an immersive experience where art and nature coalesce, making it a destination that transcends the conventional boundaries of a traditional museum.

One of the highlights of my visit was the Amphitheater, an elliptical space surrounded by ancient statues and adorned with an Egyptian obelisk. This grandiose setting once hosted Medici festivities, and standing in its midst, I could almost envision the opulent gatherings of the past. The Boboli Gardens, with its timeless charm, allows visitors to step into the pages of history.

As the day unfolded, I found myself drawn to the Grotto Grande, a hidden cave adorned with stalactite-like formations. This whimsical retreat within the gardens exudes an air of mystery, a secret chamber that adds an element of intrigue to the overall experience. It's these unexpected discoveries that make the Boboli Gardens a treasure trove for those willing to wander off the beaten path.

In the heart of the gardens lies the Fountain of Neptune, a grandiose sculpture that commands attention. As water cascaded from the mighty trident of the sea god, I couldn't help but admire the artistry that defines this outdoor masterpiece. It's a testament to the Renaissance spirit that permeates every corner of Florence, even in its hidden enclaves.

The Boboli Gardens are not merely a static attraction but a living canvas that changes with the seasons. Spring blankets the gardens in a riot of colors, with flowers in full bloom, while autumn transforms the landscape into a mosaic of warm hues. Every visit promises a new experience, as the gardens evolve through the ebb and flow of nature's rhythm.

To fully appreciate the Boboli Gardens, one must allocate sufficient time for unhurried exploration. The network of paths, alcoves, and terraces beckons visitors to lose themselves in the charm of this green retreat. Whether it's a leisurely stroll along the Viottolone or a contemplative moment by the Fountain of Bacchus, the gardens invite introspection and connection with both nature and history.

As I reluctantly bid farewell to the Boboli Gardens, I couldn't help but reflect on the privilege of having discovered this hidden gem. It's a testament to the allure of Florence, a city that extends beyond its renowned landmarks.

The Boboli Gardens, with its timeless beauty and historical resonance, stands as a reminder that sometimes, the most captivating destinations are those quietly waiting to be explored.

• San Miniato al Monte

Nestled atop the hills overlooking Florence, San Miniato al Monte stands as a hidden gem, offering a unique escape from the bustling streets below. As I ventured beyond the well-trodden paths of Florence, this medieval masterpiece unfolded before me, revealing its rich history and breathtaking beauty.

Perched on Monte alle Croci, this Romanesque basilica dates back to the 11th century and boasts a timeless elegance that often eludes the hurried traveler. The journey to San Miniato itself is an adventure, as I wound my way through narrow cobblestone streets, leaving the tourist-heavy areas behind. The anticipation built with every step, knowing that I was about to discover a side of Florence often overlooked.

Upon reaching the summit, the reward was immediate. San Miniato al Monte's façade, adorned with green and white marble, glistened in the sunlight, a prelude to the artistic treasures within. Stepping through the entrance, I was greeted by the scent of ancient stone and the soft echoes of centuries past.

The interior, a testament to Florentine craftsmanship, unfolded in a symphony of colors and forms. Intricate frescoes adorned the walls, depicting scenes from the life of Saint Miniato, the hermit upon whose burial site the basilica was built. As I wandered through the nave, the interplay of light and shadow danced upon the marble columns, creating an ethereal atmosphere that transported me to another era.

One of the highlights of San Miniato al Monte is the stunning mosaic that graces the apse. This masterpiece, created in the 13th century, narrates the coronation of the Virgin Mary, a narrative brought to life by the shimmering tiles that have withstood the test of time. It's a testament to the enduring skill of the artisans who crafted it, leaving me in awe of their talent and dedication.

The hidden gem status of San Miniato al Monte is further emphasized by the serene atmosphere that envelopes the basilica. Unlike the crowded spaces of Florence's more famous landmarks, here, I found tranquility. The soft hum of prayer resonated in the air as locals and visitors alike took a moment for quiet reflection. It's a space where the frenetic energy of the city below dissipates, allowing one to connect with the spiritual and historical essence of Florence.

The exterior of the basilica is equally captivating. The terrace in front offers panoramic views of Florence, a reward for those who make the ascent. The iconic red-tiled roofs, the meandering Arno River, and the imposing Florence Cathedral in the distance all come into focus, providing a new perspective on a city steeped in art and culture. This vantage point is a photographer's dream, capturing the essence of Florence in a single frame.

San Miniato al Monte isn't just a religious site; it's a living testament to the evolution of Florentine architecture. The adjoining cemetery, a serene final resting place for prominent Florentine families, is a showcase of funerary art spanning centuries. Intricately carved tombstones and elegant sculptures dot the landscape, creating a unique outdoor museum that pays homage to both the famous and the forgotten.

In my explorations, I stumbled upon the Chapel of the Crucifix, a small yet powerful space adorned with frescoes by Taddeo Gaddi. The emotion captured in the scenes of the Passion of Christ is palpable, creating an intimate connection between the observer and the sacred narrative. It's moments like these that make San Miniato al Monte not just a hidden gem but a trove of artistic treasures waiting to be discovered.

As I descended from the heights of San Miniato, I couldn't help but feel a sense of gratitude for stumbling upon this hidden gem. Florence, with its iconic landmarks and renowned museums, can be overwhelming in its cultural richness. Yet, in the quiet corners of the city, places like San Miniato al Monte offer respite and a chance to delve into the heart of Florence's history and artistry.

- **Oltrarno District**

The Oltrarno District, tucked away from Florence's busy streets, is a hidden treasure that visitors looking for a true Italian experience should not miss. I couldn't help but feel awe and magic as I started my tour through this quaint neighbourhood.

The Oltrarno District, which is tucked away on the south bank of the Arno River, is a peaceful haven that skillfully captures the spirit of Florence's rich cultural heritage. Oltrarno's small cobblestone lanes, where every step reveals stories from centuries past, enthral visitors in contrast to the more tourist-heavy neighbourhoods on the other side of the river.

As I meandered through the maze-like passageways, I came across artisan workshops where generations of people have been perfecting their crafts. As I walked by historic workshops where talented artists painstakingly manufactured handmade goods, the smell of leather filled the air. Oltrarno's artisans put their love and care into everything they create, from custom leather items to elaborate jewellery, creating one-of-a-kind treasures.

Oltrarno would not be the same without the Palazzo Pitti, a magnificent Renaissance castle that presides over the neighbourhood with a regal air. I was astounded by the enormous collection of artwork and historical relics kept inside as soon as I walked through its elegant hallways. I found a peaceful haven where I could see the exquisitely tended landscapes and sculptures at the Boboli Gardens, a vast green haven that stretches behind the palace.

Oltrarno's food scene proved to be a wonderful surprise for those looking for something different from the conventional Tuscan fare. Charming trattorias were scattered along the streets, serving a variety of foods made using materials that could be found nearby. Every meal, from hearty pasta dishes to succulent seafood, demonstrated the district's dedication to maintaining authentic Italian flavours.

I was lured to Piazzale Michelangelo as nightfall approached. It's a panoramic patio that sits atop a hill on the Oltrarno side. The renowned landmarks in Florence were bathed in a warm glow as the sun sank, providing a stunning perspective of the city. It was the perfect spot to take in the ageless beauty of the city without having to cope with the throngs of people that swarm the more well-liked overlooks.

Oltrarno is genuinely unique because of its sense of community and genuineness. In contrast to the tourist-heavy districts on the other side of the river, this district embodies the idea of "La Dolce Vita." People from the area walked slowly down the streets, greeting each other warmly and telling each other stories. It was a peek into the centre of Florence, where the cobblestone streets echoed with the sound of daily life.

The numerous tiny galleries hidden throughout Oltrarno's corners will comfort art lovers. These small exhibition venues offer a wide variety of modern and traditional artworks, giving up-and-coming artists a forum to express their ideas. It's evidence of the district's dedication to supporting a thriving cultural scene off the beaten path.

It seems clear to me now that Oltrarno captures the essence of Florence when I think back on my stay there. It's a location where art, history, and daily life all come together to provide a really authentic experience that goes beyond the usual tourist itinerary. I found a Florence that had not been affected by time in

Oltrarno—a secret treasure for those who are ready to go from the usual route.

• The Vasari Corridor

Tucked away in the centre of Florence, the Vasari Corridor is a secret passageway that reveals the city's rich artistic and historical heritage. When I came upon this architectural wonder, my trip through Florence's picturesque alleyways took an unexpected turn. A secret treasure waiting to be discovered, the Vasari Corridor is tucked away from the busy masses.

The wealthy Medici family commissioned Giorgio Vasari to build the corridor in 1565 as a private access point between the Palazzo Pitti and the Palazzo Vecchio. This covered walkway, which is more than a km long, enables the Medici kings to move between their homes in secrecy and stay away from the general public. Through this corridor, one feels as though they are walking in the shoes of the elite of the Renaissance; it is a journey that cuts beyond time and provides a singular viewpoint on Florence's past.

In addition to providing a physical link between two opulent homes, the Vasari Corridor is home to a remarkable art collection. Imagine strolling through a striking collection of paintings and self-portraits created by well-known artists like Velázquez, Rembrandt, and Delacroix. The hallway functions as a secret gallery, offering a close-up view of works of art that tell historical stories.

The Vasari Corridor's unique structure is one of its main draws. The famous mediaeval bridge, Ponte Vecchio, which is surrounded by jewellery stores, is crossed by the passageway. The windows along the corridor provide a captivating display of the Arno River, perfectly encapsulating the beauty of Florence. For those who are lucky enough to find it, this vantage point offers a really hidden gem—a distinct and exclusive perspective on the metropolis.

The corridor is a mystery enclave within Florence's architectural tapestry because secrecy is woven into its architecture. The entrance, which is tucked away in the Uffizi Gallery, gives the experience a sense of exclusivity. I felt privileged to have discovered this modest doorway, as though I had discovered a carefully kept secret. The Vasari Corridor invites visitors to set out on a covert journey and reveals a side of Florence best left to the inquisitive and discriminating.

The historical relevance of the Vasari Corridor goes beyond its aesthetic and architectural value. It is evidence of the power struggles and political intrigue that moulded Florence during the Renaissance. Recognised for their power in the arts, business, and politics, the Medici family used this passageway to subtly establish their dominance. It is as though you are entering a living history book, a story that comes to life with every step as you stroll along the same path that was previously echoed by the Medici monarchs' footsteps.

Because entrance to the Vasari Corridor is restricted, visiting it calls for some preparation. Guided tours, which are frequently scheduled through the Uffizi Gallery, offer a carefully crafted experience that reveals details about the history of the hallway and the backstories of the artwork hanging therein. The Vasari Corridor is still off the usual route, but exploring its hidden treasures will definitely pay off in the form of a deeper appreciation of Florence's cultural legacy.

Flowing along the cramped corridors and taking in the view of the city beyond the windows, I couldn't help but feel a connection to the historical personalities and artists who had once passed through these same hallways. A secret thread interlacing Florence's complex tapestry, the Vasari Corridor serves as a link between the past and the present.

The Vasari Corridor, amidst Florence's well-known sites and busy piazzas, is a symbol of the city's rich cultural heritage and multifaceted past. It is a secret treasure that welcomes visitors to learn the tales that are kept behind its walls, offering a special and private look into Florence's past. As I came to the end of my trip along the Vasari Corridor, I was astounded by how this undiscovered gem had deepened my awareness of Florence and permanently altered my travel experience.

CHAPTER FIVE

Culinary Delights

• Traditional Tuscan Cuisine

Florence, the heart of Tuscany, captivates not only with its art and architecture but also with its rich culinary heritage. As I strolled through the cobbled streets, the aroma of traditional Tuscan cuisine beckoned me to explore the culinary delights that define this enchanting city.

Florentine Classics:

My culinary journey began with the iconic dish - Bistecca alla Fiorentina. This massive T-bone steak, seasoned simply with salt, pepper, and a drizzle of olive oil, is a carnivore's dream. Cooked to perfection, it embodies the simplicity and authenticity of Tuscan cooking.

In the heart of Florence, I discovered another local favorite - Ribollita. This hearty soup, a medley of vegetables, beans, and bread, reflects Tuscan resourcefulness. Simmered to perfection, it's a comforting dish that warms the soul on a cool evening.

Pasta Galore:

As a pasta enthusiast, Florence unveiled a myriad of pasta dishes, each with its unique flair. Pappardelle al Cinghiale, wide ribbons of pasta adorned with a rich wild boar ragu, offered a taste of the region's rustic charm. The melding of flavors showcased the Tuscan commitment to using fresh, high-quality ingredients.

Moving beyond the classics, I delved into Pici, a thick, hand-rolled spaghetti-like pasta. It served as the perfect canvas for the robust flavors of Tuscan sauces, from aglione, a garlic and tomato sauce, to the indulgent truffle-infused variations.

Antipasti Affair:

No Tuscan meal is complete without a tantalizing array of antipasti. I reveled in the simplicity of Crostini di Fegato, toasted bread crowned with a luscious chicken liver pâté. The burst of flavors was a prelude to the culinary symphony that awaited.

Mozzarella di Bufala, paired with fresh tomatoes and basil, showcased the region's commitment to preserving culinary traditions. Each bite transported me to the sun-kissed hills of Tuscany, where artisanal cheese-making has been perfected over generations.

Divine Dolci:

Florence's sweet offerings were a delightful finale to my gastronomic escapade. Cantucci, almond biscuits typically enjoyed with Vin Santo, encapsulated the essence of Tuscan sweetness. The satisfying crunch of the biscuit paired harmoniously with the honeyed notes of the dessert wine.

Delving deeper, I discovered Schiacciata alla Fiorentina, a citrus-infused sponge cake adorned with the city's emblem - the fleur-de-lis. Its light texture and subtle sweetness provided the perfect conclusion to my Tuscan culinary adventure.

Wine Wonderland:

To complement the flavors, I ventured into the world of Tuscan wines. The robust reds, such as Chianti Classico, sang harmoniously with the bold flavors of Tuscan cuisine. The vine-covered hills that produce these wines are not just landscapes but living testaments to the region's viticultural excellence.

The Art of Aperitivo:

In Florence, the ritual of aperitivo takes on an elevated status. Sipping on a negroni or enjoying a spritz by the Arno River, I experienced the social aspect of Tuscan gastronomy. It's not just about the drinks but the camaraderie, the laughter, and the shared appreciation for life's simple pleasures.

Market Magic:

My culinary exploration wouldn't be complete without a visit to Mercato Centrale. The bustling market is a kaleidoscope of colors, aromas, and flavors. Here, I engaged with local vendors, sampling pecorino cheese, procuring fresh produce, and immersing myself in the vibrant tapestry of Tuscan ingredients.

- **Must-Try Restaurants**

In addition to being a historical and artistic mecca, Florence is also well-known for its superb food. Enjoy the following must-try restaurants, each of which offers a distinctive culinary experience, as you meander along its cobblestone streets.

1. A Culinary Time Capsule: Il Latini
Tucked away in the centre of Florence, Il Latini is a monument to authentic Tuscan cooking. This restaurant welcomes patrons to enjoy age-old recipes that have been handed down through the centuries with its rustic appeal and communal tables. The soul-warming ribollita and the recognisable Bistecca alla Fiorentina are just two examples of how Il Latini embodies Tuscan flavours.

2. The Locals' Haven: Osteria Santo Spirito
Explore the Oltrarno neighbourhood across the Arno River to find Osteria Santo Spirito, a neighbourhood treasure that residents consider to be a hidden gem. This charming restaurant embraces minimalism so that the excellence of its ingredients can be highlighted. For a true

Florentine dining experience, try the handcrafted pasta dishes and match them with a few wines from their carefully chosen list.

3. Antico Vinaio: A Paradise for Paninis

Get a delicious yet speedy bite at All'Antico Vinaio, which is close to the Uffizi Gallery. This modest sandwich store is well-known for its enormous paninis, which are stuffed to the brim with premium, freshly-sourced ingredients. Accompany both locals and visitors in line to have a taste of Florentine street food culture.

4. La Giostra: An Experience of Royal Dining

La Giostra, a hidden gem close to the Bargello Museum, provides a royal dining experience in an atmosphere evoking a bygone period. This restaurant, which combines Austrian and Italian flavours, is owned by nobility. Savour their famous ravioli of pears and pecorino while allowing the atmosphere to take you back in time to a more refined and elegant period.

5. Trattoria Sostanza: Cosy Comfort of Home

Trattoria Sostanza is the place to go if you're craving comfort food that tastes like home. This trattoria, established more than a century ago in Florence, is well-known for its food, which features a lot of butter. The well-known chicken fried in sizzling butter is a must-try recipe that has withstood the test of time and never fails to please even the pickiest eaters.

Remember that each restaurant in Florence serves as a portal to the city's rich cultural tapestry as well as a place to dine when you set out on your culinary adventure. These eating options, which range from hidden treasures to ancient buildings, will surely add a delicious chapter to your exploration of this charming Italian city..

- **Street Food Recommendations**

Discovering the thriving street food scene in Florence is a delightful way to experience the city's rich culinary history. Enticing fragrances led me to uncover a multitude of delicious goodies as I strolled around the picturesque cobblestone alleyways. Here are street foods you should definitely try while visiting this Renaissance treasure.

1. *"Perfection of Panini"*
Start your culinary journey with the famous

panini of Florence. Go to the storied sandwich store "All'Antico Vinaio," which is tucked away close to the Uffizi Gallery. Even if the lines are long, the wait is worthwhile. Choose "La Favolosa" for a delicious fusion of pecorino cheese, truffle cream, and porchetta. This culinary marvel receives the ideal crunch from the freshly cooked and crispy bread.

2. *Truffles' Triumph:*
Street food in Florence is just as famous for its truffle-infused delicacies as it is for its cuisine. Look for vendors selling truffle-flavoured popcorn or truffle-infused fries. These travel-friendly truffle treats offer a reasonably priced option to enjoy this fine treat while meandering through the charming streets of the city.

3. *Gelato Sweet Surrender:*
Gelato is a must-have for cooling off, and Florence is home to some of Italy's best gelaterias. For their delicious stracciatella and pistachio flavours, visit "Gelateria dei Neri". It is a delightful treat on a warm Florentine day because of its creamy texture and strong flavours.

4. *Delicious Fried Food: Lampredotto and Coccoli:*

Try "coccoli" (fried dough balls) for a taste of the street cuisine; they are typically served with prosciutto and stracchino cheese. This is a delicious street-side snack that is served at numerous restaurants. Try lampredotto, a classic Florentine dish prepared from a cow's fourth stomach, if you're feeling very daring. Go to the San Lorenzo market to have a real encounter.

5. Pizza al Taglio: A Slice of Heaven:

Florence may not have invented pizza, but it does have a distinctive take on this well-loved meal. Stop at "Pugi" near Santa Maria Novella to have a slice of pizza al taglio, which are rectangular slices sold by weight. It's a tasty and convenient street food alternative because of the variety of toppings and the light, fluffy crust.

6. Filosofia Fantasy:

Savour the elegance and simplicity of a flawlessly made focaccia. "Pasticceria Il Forno" provides a selection of focaccia alternatives, ranging from traditional olive to cheese and tomato. This is the perfect snack to have while taking in the architectural marvels of the city.

7. Chocolato Caldo, Chocolate Bliss:

Enjoy a rich, velvety cup of cioccolato caldo to satisfy your sweet taste. "Rivoire," a classic café in Piazza della Signoria, is well-known for its opulent rendition. When paired with a light pastry, it will send you into a chocolate-induced trance.

8. Delicious Classics: Panino con Lampredotto and Porchetta:

Savour porchetta, slow-roasted pork with flavorful herbs, for a taste of authentically Tuscan street cuisine. "Nerbone" is a well-liked location in the San Lorenzo market. Instead, sample the "panino con lampredotto," a sandwich made with tripe that has been cooked slowly, and get in touch with the local way of life. Although it's an acquired taste, the gastronomic adventure is worthwhile.

9. Cannucci-Biscotti Bliss:

Start your street food adventure with some sweet cantucci, which are almond biscuits from Tuscany. To get the real deal, try them with the sweet dessert wine Vin Santo. These crispy treats are a great way to send home a memento and can be found in many bakeries.

10. Drink and Enjoy—Pre-dinner Hour:

Enjoy the Italian custom of aperitivo as the sun

sets over the Arno River. Visit "Le Volpi e L'Uva," a quaint wine bar close to Ponte Vecchio, to enjoy a glass of local wine with cured meats and artisanal cheeses. It's the ideal way to relax following a full day of food exploration.

CHAPTER SIX

Shopping in Florence

•Florence's Markets

One of the most enchanting aspects of this Italian gem is its bustling markets, where the heart of Florence beats with the rhythm of commerce and community.

Mercato Centrale: A Culinary Wonderland

As I strolled through Florence, the Mercato Centrale emerged as a culinary haven. Nestled in the San Lorenzo district, this market is a celebration of gastronomic delights. The ground floor, a symphony of colors and aromas, showcases an array of fresh produce, from plump tomatoes to fragrant herbs. Vendors passionately share stories of their locally sourced ingredients, creating a sensory experience that immerses you in the region's agricultural richness.

Venturing upstairs, the Mercato Centrale transforms into a gastronomic playground. The air is infused with the enticing scents of Tuscan cuisine – a medley of garlic, olive oil, and simmering sauces. Artisanal pasta, cured meats, and wheels of aged cheese beckon from every corner. I couldn't resist indulging in a freshly made panino, crafted before my eyes with ingredients sourced just steps away. Each bite was a symphony of flavors, a testament to the market's commitment to authenticity.

San Lorenzo Market: Craftsmanship Unveiled

A short walk from the Mercato Centrale, the San Lorenzo Market beckons with its stalls brimming with handmade crafts. This market, in the shadow of the historic San Lorenzo Basilica, is a treasure trove of leather goods, textiles, and intricate jewelry. As I navigated through the maze of stalls, artisans proudly showcased their skills, inviting me to touch and appreciate the craftsmanship behind each piece.

Leather goods, a Florentine specialty, stole the spotlight. From supple bags to finely crafted jackets, the market offered a glimpse into Florence's rich tradition of leather craftsmanship. I couldn't resist acquiring a handmade leather journal, a tangible memento of the city's artistic heritage. The San Lorenzo Market proved to be not just a shopping destination but a voyage through the artistry that defines Florence.

Sant'Ambrogio Market: A Local's Haven

For an authentic glimpse into Florentine daily life, I explored the Sant'Ambrogio Market, a local gem tucked away from the tourist crowds. This market exudes a sense of community, where Florentines gather to purchase their daily provisions. The lively banter of vendors, the vibrant array of seasonal fruits and vegetables, and the aroma of freshly baked bread create an immersive experience into the city's everyday rhythm.

The market's diversity extends beyond food. Artisans showcase handmade goods, from ceramics to clothing, embodying the essence of local craftsmanship. Engaging in conversations with the vendors revealed not only the stories behind their products but also insights into the city's pulse. Sant'Ambrogio Market became a cherished memory, providing a genuine encounter with Florence beyond its renowned landmarks.

The Oltrarno Markets: Bohemian Elegance

Crossing the Arno River into the Oltrarno district unveiled a different facet of Florence's markets. Here, the Piazza Santo Spirito hosts a weekly market, inviting locals and visitors alike to explore a curated selection of art, antiques, and vintage finds. The bohemian atmosphere adds a touch of elegance to the shopping experience, making it a favorite haunt for those seeking unique treasures.

Wandering through the Oltrarno markets felt like stepping into an open-air gallery. Artists displayed their creations beneath the Tuscan sun, from captivating paintings to handcrafted jewelry. Antique enthusiasts reveled in the opportunity to unearth hidden gems, each piece with a story to tell. The Oltrarno markets embodied a blend of history and modernity, creating a dynamic space where tradition and innovation harmoniously coexist.

In the tapestry of Florence's markets, each thread tells a story – a narrative woven with the richness of local traditions, the artistry of craftsmanship, and the vibrant pulse of daily life. From the culinary spectacle of the Mercato Centrale to the artisanal showcase at San Lorenzo Market, the local charm of Sant'Ambrogio, and the bohemian elegance of the Oltrarno markets, Florence's markets offer a kaleidoscope of experiences.

Exploring these markets is not just a shopping excursion; it's a journey through the soul of Florence. As I reflect on my time amidst the stalls and bustling alleys, I realize that these markets are not merely places to buy and sell – they are living narratives, inviting each visitor to become a part of Florence's timeless tale.

- **High-end Boutiques**

In the heart of Florence, high-end boutiques adorn the historic streets, weaving a tapestry of luxury amidst the city's rich cultural fabric. As I strolled through this Renaissance gem, the allure of these exclusive shops beckoned, promising a unique blend of fashion, craftsmanship, and Italian sophistication.

One cannot talk about luxury shopping in Florence without mentioning the iconic Via Tornabuoni. This renowned street is a runway of opulence, lined with elite boutiques that showcase the epitome of Italian style. The polished windows of Gucci, Prada, and Salvatore Ferragamo reflect the city's commitment to fashion excellence. Each step on Via Tornabuoni is a journey through sartorial elegance, as the boutiques here curate a selection of haute couture and timeless accessories that redefine luxury.

Wandering further into Florence's intricate labyrinth, I discovered the historic Antico Setificio Fiorentino. Nestled near the Arno River, this boutique weaves a narrative of tradition and craftsmanship dating back to the 18th century. As I traced the delicate threads of silk, the artisans' dedication to preserving ancient weaving techniques became evident. Here, bespoke fabrics whisper tales of a bygone era, offering visitors a chance to immerse themselves in the artistry that defines Florence.

For those seeking not just fashion, but a fusion of art and design, the Luisa Via Roma concept store is a must-visit. Housed in a medieval palace, this avant-garde space transcends conventional boundaries. As I explored its curated sections, I encountered a dynamic convergence of high fashion, contemporary art, and lifestyle. Luisa Via Roma is not merely a boutique; it is a cultural crossroads where the past and present collide in a kaleidoscope of creativity.

In the shadows of Florence's architectural marvels, the Stefano Ricci boutique stands as a testament to unparalleled luxury in menswear. The craftsmanship and attention to detail in each piece are nothing short of extraordinary. From impeccably tailored suits to accessories that exude refinement, Stefano Ricci's creations redefine the concept of sartorial elegance. The boutique itself, with its regal ambiance, reflects the brand's commitment to timeless sophistication.

As I delved deeper into the city's fashion scene, the Officina Profumo-Farmaceutica di Santa Maria Novella emerged as a fragrant oasis. Established in the 17th century as a pharmacy, this boutique now boasts an exquisite collection of perfumes, skincare, and home fragrances. Stepping into this olfactory haven felt like a sensory journey through time, with each product crafted using ancient recipes that have withstood centuries.

While Florence's high-end boutiques weave a narrative of luxury, the Oltrarno district introduces a different facet of artisanal charm.

Here, tucked away from the bustling crowds, I stumbled upon ateliers where skilled craftsmen meticulously create leather goods. From hand-stitched leather bags to custom-made shoes, these workshops offer an intimate glimpse into the artistry that defines Florentine leather craftsmanship.

In the pursuit of unique treasures, the Ponte Vecchio emerges as a beacon of timeless allure. Beyond its historical significance, this bridge is home to jewelry boutiques that showcase the finest Italian craftsmanship. The sparkle of exquisite jewels in family-owned stores adds a touch of romance to the air, inviting visitors to indulge in the art of adornment.

As the sun dipped below Florence's iconic skyline, my journey through high-end boutiques became a symphony of experiences. From the grandeur of Via Tornabuoni to the intimate workshops of Oltrarno, each boutique echoed the city's commitment to preserving its artistic legacy. In Florence, luxury is not just a transaction; it is a cultural exchange where the past converges with the present, creating a tapestry of opulence that transcends time.

• Local Artisans and Crafts

Discovering Florence's exquisite handicrafts is like taking a trip back in time, as the city's craftsmen bring venerable customs to life. Thanks to the talented hands of its artisans, I found myself wandering the cobblestone streets and discovering a city where art isn't just found in museums but penetrates every corner.

Time seems to stand still in the artisan workshops of Florence, an attraction that is impossible to resist. Entering these ateliers is akin to opening a portal to another period. The soft buzz of looms creating elaborate patterns and the rhythmic sounds of hammers shaping metal fill the air. Every workshop bears witness to the painstaking workmanship that has been inherited over the years.

Nestled on the south bank of the Arno River, the Oltrarno area is one such hidden gem. Offering a window into the essence of Florence's handmade heritage, this enclave serves as a sanctuary for artists and craftspeople. The smell of freshly worked leather filled the air as I walked down the tiny streets. Florence's legacy is deeply ingrained in leathercraft, and the world's best leather goods are created in these workshops.

One of the best examples is the Florence Leather School, or Scuola del Cuoio. Established following World War II, this establishment has come to represent superior leather crafting. Guests may watch as skilled craftspeople painstakingly create wallets, purses, and other leather goods, exhibiting a tasteful fusion of innovation and tradition. The sound of tools against hides and the lingering smell of tanned leather combine to produce an immersive experience that goes beyond simple observation.

The famous San Lorenzo Market in the centre of Florence is laid out like a colourful tapestry of textures and colours. Local craftspeople invite onlookers to explore the realm of Florentine craftsmanship by exhibiting their items with pride in this location. Eye-catching pieces include ceramics, textiles, and elaborate jewellery, each of which conveys a tale of artistry and devotion.

The small workshops dotted around Florence are a sanctuary for the delicate craft of ceramics. It's fascinating to see expert potters form clay into beautiful shapes. At the Della

Robbia family workshop, where a tradition of ceramicists has been creating masterpieces since the fifteenth century, I could not help but be drawn. Their ceramic masterpieces' vivid colours and elaborate motifs are a reflection of Florence's innate artistic richness.

Florence is also a city rich in textile history, as the city's weavers continue to practice the craft of producing beautiful textiles. This tradition is exemplified by the Antico Setificio Fiorentino, a historic silk workshop. I was in awe of the commitment to maintaining age-old methods as I ran my fingertips over the opulent silks. Hand-turned looms reverberated throughout the facility, emphasising the dedication to producing fabrics of unmatched quality.

A thorough examination of Florence's artisanal scene would be incomplete without a look at the paper industry. The exquisite craft of hand-decorated papers is on display in the well-known paper workshop, Il Papiro. Notebooks, stationery, and ornamental objects are adorned with intricate designs and vivid hues that provide a concrete link to Florence's artistic past.

Florence's artisanal spirit reaches into the culinary arts in addition to the tangible crafts.

A sensory extravaganza, the Mercato Centrale is a busy market located in the centre of the city. The gastronomic gems of the area are displayed here by regional producers and craftspeople. Every stand conveys a story of passion for food as an art form, from the savoury tastes of handmade cheeses to the fragrant oils steeped in truffle.

The Ponte Vecchio is a well-known representation of Florence's goldsmithing heritage in the world of jewellery. The jewellery stores that line the old bridge are decked up with priceless items that sparkle in their windows. I was enthralled with the glittering exhibits as I strolled across the bridge; each one was a tribute to the city's unwavering devotion to fine craftsmanship.

Not only do Florence's artists create things, but they also look after a legacy of culture. Their ateliers and workshops serve as living museums, maintaining customs that have shaped the city for many years. Florence showed itself to me as a living canvas where the past and present fluidly blend together, allowing tourists to be a part of an enduring artistic journey as I immersed myself in the world of local artisans and crafts.

CHAPTER SEVEN

Day Trips from Florence

- **Siena**

Siena, a captivating city nestled in the heart of Tuscany, beckons travelers seeking a taste of medieval charm within a day's reach from Florence. As I embarked on my day trip from Florence to Siena, I found myself enchanted by its narrow winding streets, stunning architecture, and the palpable sense of history that permeates the air.

Departing from Florence, the scenic drive to Siena sets the stage for the day's adventure. The undulating hills adorned with vineyards and olive groves provide a picturesque backdrop, preparing visitors for the architectural wonders that await in Siena's historic center.

Upon arrival, my first stop was the Piazza del Campo, Siena's iconic shell-shaped square. This medieval masterpiece is not merely a physical space but a testament to Siena's rich cultural and communal heritage. The Torre del Mangia, soaring high above the square, offers panoramic views of the city and its surroundings. Climbing to its summit, I marveled at the patchwork of terracotta roofs and the distant rolling hills, gaining a profound appreciation for Siena's strategic and aesthetic significance.

The heart of Siena, however, lies in its medieval streets. Wandering through the narrow alleys, I discovered hidden gems, from quaint cafes serving authentic Tuscan cuisine to artisanal shops showcasing local craftsmanship. The Duomo di Siena, a masterpiece of Italian Gothic architecture, stands as a testament to the city's religious devotion and artistic prowess. Its facade, adorned with intricate sculptures and mosaics, drew me into a world where every detail tells a story.

In the cathedral's interior, the Piccolomini Library houses exquisite frescoes by Pinturicchio, transporting visitors to a bygone era of opulence and patronage. The breathtaking mosaic floor, unveiled only during certain months, is a testament to Siena's commitment to preserving and sharing its artistic heritage.

As I continued my exploration, I stumbled upon the Contrade, the 17 neighborhoods that form the social fabric of Siena. Each Contrada boasts its own unique identity, symbolized by distinct emblems and colors. The palpable sense of civic pride and competition is most evident during the renowned Palio di Siena, a biannual horse race that transforms the Piazza del Campo into a pulsating arena of tradition and rivalry.

Siena's culinary offerings are a feast for the senses. I relished in a leisurely lunch at a local trattoria, savoring regional specialties such as pappa al pomodoro, ribollita, and pici pasta. The robust flavors, paired with a glass of Chianti Classico, highlighted the gastronomic delights that define Tuscan cuisine.

Immersing myself further into Siena's cultural tapestry, I visited the Civic Museum, housed in the Palazzo Pubblico. The museum's collection spans centuries, featuring masterpieces by Sienese artists such as Simone Martini and Ambrogio Lorenzetti. The frescoes in the Sala della Pace (Room of Peace) offer a thought-provoking commentary on governance, justice, and the pursuit of a harmonious society.

Before concluding my day in Siena, I embraced the leisurely pace of life with a passeggiata along the city walls. The panoramic views of the Tuscan countryside and the distant silhouette of Siena provided a fitting finale to a day filled with cultural immersion and sensory delights.

As the sun dipped below the horizon, casting a warm glow over the city, I reflected on the seamless blend of history, art, and culinary experiences that define Siena. My day trip from Florence had not only enriched my understanding of Tuscany's cultural tapestry but had also left an indelible imprint of Siena's timeless allure.

In retrospect, Siena stands as a testament to the enduring spirit of medieval Italy, inviting modern travelers to step back in time and witness the beauty of a bygone era. For those exploring Florence, a day trip to Siena is not just a geographical excursion but a journey through the pages of history, art, and tradition.

- **Pisa**

In Florence, embarking on a day trip to Pisa is a captivating journey through the heart of Tuscany. The iconic Leaning Tower of Pisa awaits, a testament to architectural marvels that have stood the test of time. As I ventured beyond Florence's enchanting cityscape, the allure of Pisa beckoned with its rich history and picturesque landscapes.

The journey from Florence to Pisa is a seamless blend of convenience and scenic beauty. Opting for a comfortable train ride from Santa Maria Novella station, I found myself immersed in the Tuscan countryside within an hour. The rolling hills, dotted with vineyards and olive groves, create a visual symphony that sets the tone for the day's exploration.

Upon reaching Pisa, the Piazza dei Miracoli unfolds, a UNESCO World Heritage Site that houses the iconic Leaning Tower, the Cathedral, and the Baptistery. Standing on the vast expanse of the square, the Leaning Tower's distinctive tilt becomes immediately apparent, sparking curiosity and awe. As I delved into the intricate details of its construction, the history and engineering marvels unfolded before my eyes.

Climbing the Leaning Tower is a unique experience, offering panoramic views of Pisa and its surroundings. The gradual ascent allows for reflection on the tower's precarious lean and the architectural ingenuity that preserved its stability for centuries. The panorama from the top showcases the Arno River winding through the landscape, connecting Pisa to the broader tapestry of Tuscany.

Exploring the Piazza dei Miracoli extends beyond the Leaning Tower. The Pisa Cathedral, a masterpiece of Romanesque architecture, beckons with its ornate facade and stunning interior. The Baptistery, a cylindrical structure adjacent to the cathedral, unveils awe-inspiring acoustics that captivate visitors with harmonic resonance.

Strolling through the charming streets of Pisa, away from the Piazza dei Miracoli, reveals a town steeped in history and cultural richness. The vibrant colors of medieval buildings line the Arno River, creating a postcard-perfect setting. Quaint cafes and gelaterias offer delightful pitstops, allowing travelers to savor the local flavors and absorb the relaxed pace of life in Pisa.

For those seeking a cultural immersion beyond the architectural wonders, the Campo Santo, or monumental cemetery, is a hidden gem. Its tranquil cloisters and impressive collection of frescoes create a serene atmosphere, inviting visitors to contemplate the passage of time amidst ancient tombs and sculptures.

Pisa's charm extends beyond its historic center. A leisurely walk along the Arno River provides a different perspective, allowing glimpses of everyday life in this enchanting town. The lively atmosphere of Pisa's streets, adorned with colorful boutiques and artisan shops, adds a contemporary flair to its timeless appeal.

As the day in Pisa draws to a close, indulging in local cuisine is a must. Pisa offers a culinary journey that mirrors its diverse history. Traditional Tuscan dishes, such as ribollita and pappa al pomodoro, showcase the region's culinary heritage. Pairing these delights with a glass of Chianti wine, sourced from the nearby vineyards, completes the sensory experience.

Reflecting on my day trip from Florence to Pisa, I couldn't help but appreciate the seamless fusion of history, architecture, and natural beauty. Pisa, with its Leaning Tower as the focal point, is a testament to the enduring allure of Tuscany. Each step in this charming town unfolds layers of the past while embracing the present, making it an indispensable addition to any Florence travel itinerary.

- **Chianti Region**

Visiting the Chianti Region from Florence offers a captivating journey through the heart of Tuscany, where vineyards, olive groves, and charming villages paint a picturesque landscape. As I embarked on day trips from Florence, the allure of the Chianti Region unfolded, revealing a tapestry of flavors, history, and stunning vistas.

Our adventure began with a scenic drive, winding through the iconic Tuscan countryside. The undulating hills adorned with vineyards and cypress trees set the stage for what promised to be a quintessential Italian experience. The Chianti Region, situated between Florence and Siena, is renowned for its wine production, and our first stop reflected this heritage.

Arriving at a traditional winery, I immersed myself in the art of winemaking. Guided tours unveiled the meticulous process, from grape harvesting to fermentation and aging in oak barrels. Tasting the renowned Chianti Classico, with its distinct notes of cherry and spice, provided a sensory journey into the region's vinicultural excellence.

Continuing our exploration, we meandered through medieval villages that seemed frozen in time. Greve in Chianti, a charming market town, welcomed us with its central square, Piazza Matteotti, flanked by artisan shops and local eateries. Here, the aroma of freshly baked bread mingled with the fragrance of olive oil, inviting us to savor Tuscan culinary delights.

One cannot talk about Chianti without acknowledging the iconic vineyards of Panzano. Perched on a hill, Panzano offers panoramic views of the surrounding valleys. We indulged in a leisurely lunch at a rustic trattoria, savoring homemade pasta and locally sourced ingredients. The convivial atmosphere and robust flavors reflected the authenticity ingrained in Chianti's gastronomic culture.

The journey continued to Radda in Chianti, another gem in this medieval necklace. Its narrow streets and stone buildings exude a timeless charm, inviting exploration. Local artisans showcased their craftsmanship, from handmade ceramics to leather goods, providing an opportunity to take home a piece of Chianti's artisanal heritage.

As the day unfolded, we delved into the historical richness of Castellina in Chianti. The imposing Rocca, a medieval fortress, stood as a testament to the region's strategic significance during the Middle Ages. Walking through its cobbled streets, I marveled at the fusion of history and modern life, where ancient structures seamlessly coexist with contemporary cafes and boutiques.

A visit to Chianti is incomplete without experiencing its olive oil culture. At a family-owned olive grove, we learned about the olive oil production process, from orchard cultivation to cold-press extraction. Tasting the golden elixir, with its peppery finish and fresh, grassy notes, heightened our appreciation for this liquid gold integral to Tuscan cuisine.

The day drew to a close with a sunset drive through the vineyards, where the play of light on the landscape created a mesmerizing tableau. Back in Florence, I reflected on the enriching day spent in the Chianti Region—a journey that seamlessly blended history, gastronomy, and the art of winemaking.

Exploring the Chianti Region from Florence is a pilgrimage into the soul of Tuscany. Each village, vineyard, and olive grove contributes to a narrative that transcends time, offering travelers a glimpse into the region's rich heritage. Whether indulging in the robust flavors of Chianti Classico, wandering through medieval streets, or savoring the liquid gold of local olive oil, every moment in Chianti is a celebration of the extraordinary tapestry woven by centuries of tradition.

- **Cinque Terre**

Florence, a city steeped in art, history, and culture, offers not just the splendor of its Renaissance treasures but also serves as a gateway to the enchanting Cinque Terre. Embarking on day trips from Florence to this coastal gem is an adventure that unveils the beauty of the Ligurian coastline.

As I ventured beyond Florence's cobblestone streets, the allure of Cinque Terre beckoned. These five colorful villages – Monterosso al Mare, Vernazza, Corniglia, Manarola, and Riomaggiore – are perched along the rugged cliffs, creating a postcard-perfect panorama. A quick train ride from Florence brings you to La Spezia, the gateway to Cinque Terre.

Upon reaching La Spezia, I found myself standing at the threshold of a UNESCO World Heritage Site, a testament to the timeless charm of these coastal villages. Opting for the Cinque Terre Card, a golden ticket to explore the area's trails and hop between villages seamlessly, I set out on a journey that promised both natural beauty and a taste of local life.

Monterosso al Mare, the largest of the five, unfolded its beaches and pastel-hued houses before my eyes. The sea breeze carried the scent of salty air, and I wandered through the narrow alleys, discovering hidden trattorias serving fresh seafood. Each village offered a unique character, a kaleidoscope of colors against the azure backdrop of the Ligurian Sea.

Vernazza, with its medieval tower and picturesque harbor, invited me to linger a while. Here, I succumbed to the allure of gelato while watching fishing boats bob gently in the harbor. The coastal path connecting Vernazza to Monterosso proved a scenic trek, offering panoramic views that whispered tales of centuries past.

Corniglia, perched atop a cliff, stood as a tranquil oasis. Its terraced vineyards painted a patchwork of green against the blue sky. The absence of a direct sea access bestowed Corniglia with a peaceful ambiance, making it an ideal spot to savor local wine and absorb the tranquility of the surroundings.

Manarola's colorful buildings, seemingly stacked upon each other, greeted me like a vibrant amphitheater. As the sun dipped below the horizon, the village illuminated, casting a warm glow over the cliffs. It was a moment frozen in time, capturing the magic of Cinque Terre.

Riomaggiore, the southernmost village, charmed me with its narrow alleys and lively atmosphere. As dusk settled, I found myself at the marina, where boats gently rocked in the evening tide. The coastal trail connecting Riomaggiore to Manarola, known as the Via dell'Amore or Lover's Lane, provided a romantic stroll as the moonlit sea shimmered below.

Cinque Terre's trails are a hiker's haven, and the Sentiero Azzurro, or Blue Trail, connecting all five villages, offered a feast for the senses. From panoramic viewpoints to lush vineyards, each step unveiled a new facet of this coastal paradise. Hiking from Vernazza to Monterosso, I marveled at the sheer beauty that surrounded me, a harmonious blend of nature and human endeavor.

As I reflect on my day trips from Florence to Cinque Terre, I am left with indelible memories of a coastline etched with history, adorned with colorful villages, and embraced by the Ligurian Sea. The synergy of nature and culture in Cinque Terre is a testament to the enduring spirit of coastal life. Florence may be the cradle of the Renaissance, but Cinque Terre, with its timeless allure, is a symphony of sea and land, a melody that lingers in the heart long after the journey concludes.

CHAPTER EIGHT

Cultural Experiences

• Opera and Classical Performances

Every traveller may expect a symphony of cultural richness in Florence, the centre of Tuscany. I was enthralled with the grandeur of opera and classical performances that epitomise the city's creative soul as I meandered along the cobblestone streets.

Extravaganza Opera:
Opera is a theatrical art form that finds its inspiration in Florence, the city recognised as its birthplace. The world-famous Teatro del Maggio Musicale Fiorentino is proof of the city's love for opera. Since its founding in the 1930s, the theatre has presented performances of the highest calibre because of its magnificent architecture and extensive history.

Going to an opera at the Teatro del Maggio Musicale Fiorentino is an adventure into Florence's creative heritage as well as a cultural experience. The theatre's acoustics encompass the audience, producing a time-travelling immersive experience. Every concert turns into a celebration of the city's musical history, whether it is through the ardent arias of Giuseppe Verdi or the captivating works of Giuseppe Puccini.

Classic Superstars:

Florence's classical performances create a rich tapestry of lyrical brilliance that extends beyond the captivating world of opera. Thanks to locations like the Sala Verdi at the Conservatorio di Musica Luigi Cherubini, the city is filled with the reverberations of classical classics. From symphony concerts to solo recitals, this music venue in the centre of Florence presents a variety of classical acts.

A classical performance in Florence is a feast for the senses. The antique rooms are filled with the sound of a grand piano or the gentle notes of a violin, which takes you to another time and place. The gifted musicians exhibit a degree of expertise that reflects Florence's dedication to creative quality. They are frequently raised in the city's respected music schools.

Related Cultures:

With its extensive creative legacy, Florence acts as a crossroads of cultures where the old and the new coexist. The visual feast that is the

Uffizi Gallery, which houses works by Michelangelo, Leonardo da Vinci, and Botticelli, serves as an introduction to the city's musical grandeur. I couldn't help but envision the harmonies that once permeated the air during the Renaissance as I strolled through the gallery's halls, reflecting the feelings of a city that breathes art in every form.

With its sculptures and architectural marvels, the Piazza della Signoria turns into a venue for spontaneous street acts. The area comes to life with musicians and performers, who foster an environment where the lines between spectators and artists are blurred. These are the times when Florence's dedication to artistic expression shines through, reminding me that the city is a creative living canvas rather than just a place to visit.

Silent Jewels:
In between the popular locations, Florence has hidden areas that are home to captivating acts. With its charming atmosphere, St. Mark's English Church offers a distinctive venue for chamber music performances. The song took me to a place of breathtaking beauty as I sat in the pews in the warm glow of candlelight.

My investigation into Florence's music scene also brought me to the Teatro Niccolini, a hidden treasure with a charming old-world aura. Hidden away from the busy streets, this small theatre presents a range of events, including musical showcases and classical plays. Experiencing a performance here is akin to unearthing a closely guarded secret—an honour that links you to the real pulse of Florence's cultural beating heart.

Gastronomic Harmonies:

Without partaking in Florence's delectable cuisine, no study of its cultural tapestry is complete. At restaurants such as Ristorante del Fagioli, where mouthwatering Tuscan delicacies are served alongside live classical music, the marriage of music and cuisine is expertly arranged. The music complemented the meal experience as I relished every bite, resulting in a symphony of flavours that lingered long after the last taste.

Opera and classical music performances are more than just events in Florence; they are an integral part of the city's culture. Through the centuries-spanning tales conveyed by each note played and aria sung, this captivating city's cultural past is brought to life for contemporary enthusiasts. Florence presents itself as more than just a place to visit; it's also an eternal tribute to the harmonies of the human soul, especially when the sun sets over the Arno River and melodies linger in the air.

• Festivals and Events

Discovering Florence's rich mosaic of celebrations and activities is akin to entering a living historical chronicle. The city's great cultural diversity captivates one, and the many events that fill its calendar only serve to heighten this attraction.

1. Florence Carnival:
The vibrant Florence Carnival, a kaleidoscope of colours and enthusiasm, welcomes the city each year. The spirit of celebration fills the streets, as seen in the intricately made masks and the energetic parades. It's a time when both locals and tourists embrace Florence's fun side.

2. The Easter Holiday:
Florence offers a spiritual and artistic Easter experience. The churches in the city hold sombre processions that combine breathtaking art and holy fervour. Don't miss the

centuries-old custom known as Scoppio del Carro, in which a cart filled with pyrotechnics is set ablaze to represent a bountiful crop and wealth.

3. Fiorentino Musical Maggio:
One of the most renowned and ancient music festivals in Europe, the Maggio Musicale Fiorentino, takes place in May and is perfect for lovers of classical music. Music lovers are treated to an auditory feast as world-class performances, from symphonies to operas, take place in the city's ancient theatres.

4. Historical Cricket:
In June, the exhilarating spectacle of Calcio Storico, a mediaeval football forerunner, takes place. In Piazza Santa Croce, teams from various neighbourhoods compete in a lively and occasionally fierce match that displays not only athletic prowess but also a strong sense of community pride.

5. Festival of Florence Dance:
The Florence Dance Festival takes centre stage as the city is blessed with the summer heat. Famous dancers and choreographers come together to offer amazing shows, transforming Florence into a dance lover's brief paradise.

6. San Giovanni's Day:
Festa di San Giovanni, held on June 24th, honours St. John the Baptist, the patron saint of Florence, and is a magnificent celebration. A magnificent fireworks show over the Arno River marks the end of the day and casts a mystical glow over well-known sites like Ponte Vecchio.

7. Fiesolana Estate:
Get outside the city limits and check out Estate Fiesolana, a summertime arts festival in the quaint hamlet of Fiesole, which is close to Florence. Under the stars, concerts, plays, and movie screenings take place in the ruins of the ancient Roman theatre.

8. Florence Biennale:

Every two years, the Florence Biennale is a must-see event for art fans. This global showcase of contemporary art draws artists and enthusiasts from all over the world, converting the city into a vibrant showcase of innovative creation.

9. Tattoo Convention in Florence:
Defying convention, the September Florence Tattoo Convention gives the city's events schedule a contemporary, edgy feel. Tattoo

artists from all around the world get together to exhibit their skills and create a special blend of subculture and art.

10. *The Film Festival in Florence:*
Fans of films can enjoy the Florence Film Festival as the year comes to an end. Featuring an eclectic line-up of films ranging from avant-garde indies to global hits, this occasion offers a cinematic epilogue to Florence's cultural mosaic.

- **Florence's Art Scene**

The Renaissance's birthplace, Florence, has an enduring art scene that captivates all visitors with its depth of historical detail. Walking around the cobblestone streets, I saw how the city unveiled like a living museum, with every corner revealing a tale through its blend of architecture and art.

A must-see is the Uffizi Gallery, a veritable gold mine of treasures. It was like taking a tour through the progression of art when one was surrounded by works by Michelangelo, Botticelli, and Leonardo da Vinci. I was enthralled by Botticelli's ethereal masterpiece,

The Birth of Venus, which has captivated me for ages with its delicate beauty.

A visit to the Accademia Gallery provided a close-up view of Michelangelo's David, a massive work of art that exudes grace and strength. As I stood there, I was astounded by the sculptor's ability to bring the marble to life, which is a monument to human inventiveness.

While meandering through the alleys of Florence, I happened upon the Pitti Palace, a Renaissance treasure that houses a vast collection of artwork. The striking artwork on display was complemented by the tranquil Boboli Gardens, a sanctuary of greenery that perfectly blended culture and environment.

The street art culture in Florence is just as lively. The bohemian Santo Spirito neighbourhood offered a modern contrast to the city's traditional beauty with its vibrant murals and graffiti. By discovering these undiscovered treasures, I was able to observe Florence's vibrant artistic development.

One moving representation of Florence's artistic and historical identity has been the Basilica di Santa Croce. I entered this opulent basilica and saw the tombs of luminaries like

Michelangelo, Galileo, and Niccol Machiavelli all around me. The murals that covered the walls made the area into a moving picture that told the story of the city's cultural heritage.

Florence's open-air artwork is what makes it so charming, even if you skip the famous galleries and museums. The city's artistic past served as an inspiration for street entertainers who brought the piazzas to life. Florence's public areas became a canvas for modern artistic expression, from musicians serenading bystanders to living statues that appeared to defy time.

Investigating Oltrarno, the "other side of the Arno," showed us another aspect of Florence's artistic community. The streets were lined with artisan workshops producing beautiful, handcrafted products. I was able to see the city's artisanal legacy being preserved by seeing the traditional workmanship that has been passed down through the centuries by visiting these workshops.

A modern art exposition called the Florence Biennale demonstrated the city's dedication to supporting emerging creative voices. Events were held in galleries and other cultural venues across the city, fostering a vibrant environment that honoured both the avant-garde and the historical.

Cafés provided both a culinary and visual feast, such as the iconic Caffè Rivoire in Piazza della Signoria. With views of famous sculptures and luxurious surroundings surrounding you, sipping espresso seemed like travelling back in time to a place where conversation and art came together.

CHAPTER NINE

Practical Tips

• Transportation Tips

As I strolled through the charming streets of Florence, I quickly discovered that transportation plays a crucial role in making the most of this enchanting city. Here are some valuable tips to help you navigate Florence seamlessly.

1. Walk the Renaissance Streets:
Florence's historic city center is a treasure trove of art and architecture, and the best way to immerse yourself in its beauty is on foot. Most of the major attractions, like the Uffizi Gallery, Ponte Vecchio, and the Duomo, are within a comfortable walking distance. So, lace up your comfortable shoes and get ready to explore the Renaissance wonders that await at every turn.

2. Embrace the Two-Wheeled Culture:
For a more local experience, consider renting a bicycle. Florence is a bike-friendly city with

dedicated lanes and bike-sharing programs. Cycling allows you to cover more ground than walking while still savoring the city's atmosphere. Imagine pedaling along the Arno River, feeling the wind in your hair as you pass by picturesque landscapes.

3. Efficient Public Transportation:
Florence has a well-organized public transportation system, including buses. They are a convenient option for reaching attractions situated a bit farther from the city center. Be sure to purchase tickets in advance and familiarize yourself with the routes. The efficient bus network is an excellent way to explore the surrounding areas and hills, offering stunning views of the Tuscan countryside.

4. Hop-on, Hop-off Bus Tours:
If you want a hassle-free way to see the main sights, consider a hop-on, hop-off bus tour. These double-decker buses provide a narrated tour of the city, allowing you to explore at your own pace. Hop off when you spot something intriguing, and hop back on when you're ready to continue your adventure. It's a great way to get an overview of Florence's highlights.

5. Romantic River Cruises:

The Arno River gracefully flows through Florence, and a romantic river cruise is a unique way to experience the city's beauty. Choose a traditional barchetto or opt for a more modern boat tour. As you glide along the water, you'll have a distinctive perspective of Florence's skyline, with the sun setting behind iconic landmarks.

6. Taxis – Convenient, but Use Wisely:

Taxis are readily available in Florence and can be a convenient option, especially if you're carrying luggage or need to reach a destination quickly. However, they can be expensive, so use them judiciously. Make sure the taxi meter is running, or agree on a fare beforehand. Taxis can be found at designated stands or hailed on the street.

7. Explore Surrounding Villages:

Florence is a gateway to the charming Tuscan countryside. Consider renting a car to explore nearby villages like Fiesole, known for its Roman ruins and panoramic views. Having a car allows you the flexibility to venture into the picturesque landscapes surrounding Florence and discover hidden gems off the beaten path.

8. Train Travel – Beyond Florence:

Florence's central train station, Santa Maria Novella, connects the city to other major Italian destinations. If you're planning day trips to cities like Pisa, Siena, or even Rome, taking the train is a convenient and scenic option. High-speed trains whisk you across the Italian landscape, offering a comfortable and efficient mode of travel.

- **Safety and Health**

In Florence, safety and health are paramount considerations for any traveler. Navigating this historic city, known for its Renaissance art and architecture, becomes a richer experience when you prioritize your well-being.

Safety:

Florence is generally a safe city, but like any tourist destination, it's essential to stay vigilant. Pickpocketing can occur, especially in crowded areas like the Ponte Vecchio and the Uffizi Gallery. Utilize anti-theft measures such as money belts and be cautious with your belongings.

Traffic in Florence can be hectic, with narrow streets and a mix of pedestrians, bicycles, and vehicles. Exercise caution when crossing roads, and be aware of the local driving patterns. Stick to designated crosswalks and follow traffic signals.

For emergencies, dial 112—the universal emergency number in Italy. Familiarize yourself with the location of the nearest embassy or consulate, and keep a copy of important documents like your passport in a secure place.

Health:

Italian healthcare is generally of high quality, but it's wise to have travel insurance covering medical expenses. The European Health Insurance Card (EHIC) may be applicable for EU citizens. Locate the nearest hospital and pharmacy, and keep a list of essential medical information, including allergies and existing conditions.

Florence's tap water is safe to drink, but if you prefer bottled water, it's readily available. Italian cuisine is delightful, but be mindful of food hygiene. Choose restaurants with good reviews, and ensure that meat is thoroughly cooked. If you have dietary restrictions, communicate them clearly to the restaurant staff.

First Aid and Pharmacies:

Carry a basic first aid kit, including items like bandages, pain relievers, and any necessary prescription medications. Pharmacies in Florence are well-equipped, and pharmacists can provide assistance for minor health concerns.

Comfort and Well-being:

Exploring Florence involves a lot of walking, so wear comfortable shoes. The city's cobblestone streets can be uneven, so be cautious of your footing. During the summer, stay hydrated and protect yourself from the sun with sunscreen and a hat.

Local Health Customs:

Italians are health-conscious, and smoking is not as prevalent as in some other European countries. However, be aware that some indoor spaces may still permit smoking. If you have respiratory sensitivities, inquire about smoking policies at restaurants and accommodations.

• Local Customs to Be Aware Of

As I wandered through the enchanting streets of Florence, I quickly realized that embracing local customs is key to unlocking the true essence of this timeless city. In this guide, I'll share insights into the customs that define the Florentine way of life, helping you immerse yourself in the rich tapestry of this cultural haven.

Greetings and Social Etiquette

The Florentines take great pride in their warm and friendly demeanor. When meeting someone, a firm handshake and direct eye contact are customary. It's common to exchange pleasantries before delving into more serious conversations. Politeness is highly valued, and saying "per favore" (please) and "grazie" (thank you) goes a long way.

Dining Etiquette

Dining in Florence is not just a meal; it's an experience. When invited to someone's home, it's polite to bring a small gift, such as a bottle of wine or flowers. During meals, wait for the host to start eating before you begin. Pasta is often eaten with a fork and spoon, and it's acceptable to use bread to mop up any delicious sauces left on the plate.

Dress Code

Florentines are known for their impeccable sense of style, and it's advisable to dress neatly when exploring the city. In churches and other religious sites, modest attire is a must. Shoulders and knees should be covered, so it's a good idea to carry a scarf or shawl for such occasions.

Art and History Appreciation

Florence is a treasure trove of art and history, and locals take great pride in their cultural heritage. When visiting museums and historical sites, maintain a respectful tone and avoid loud conversations. Photography policies vary, so always check before capturing that perfect moment.

Time Management

Florence operates on a more relaxed schedule, with a lengthy midday break known as "riposo." Many businesses close during this time, so plan your activities accordingly. Additionally, punctuality is appreciated, but flexibility is equally important. A leisurely pace is the norm when strolling through the city's charming streets.

Language Considerations

While English is widely understood, making an effort to speak some Italian phrases will be warmly received. "Buongiorno" (good morning) and "buona sera" (good evening) are simple yet effective greetings. Learning a few basic phrases will enhance your interactions with locals.

Street Etiquette

The streets of Florence are a delightful maze of history and modernity. Keep in mind that walking on the left side of narrow streets allows smoother pedestrian flow. Respect queue lines and wait your turn, whether in a gelato shop or at a local market. It's these small gestures that make a big difference.

Festivals and Celebrations

Florentines are known for their vibrant festivals, such as the famous "Scoppio del Carro" during Easter. Embrace the festivities, join in the celebrations, and don't be shy to ask locals about the significance of different events. It's an excellent way to connect with the community.

CHAPTER TEN

Itinerary Suggestions

- **One Day in Florence**

For travellers with just one day to immerse myself in the wonders of this city, I crafted an itinerary that blended iconic landmarks, delectable cuisine, and a touch of local charm.

Morning: 8:00 AM - 12:00 PM

Start at Piazza del Duomo:
Begin your day in awe of Florence's iconic cathedral, the Duomo. Climb to the top for panoramic views of the city and its terracotta rooftops. The intricate details of the cathedral and the baptistery below are a testament to Florence's artistic prowess.

Uffizi Gallery:
Delve into the art world at the Uffizi Gallery. Home to masterpieces by Michelangelo, Leonardo da Vinci, and Botticelli, this gallery is a treasure trove of Renaissance art. Booking tickets in advance is advisable to skip the lines.

Lunch: 12:00 PM - 1:30 PM

Trattoria Mario:
Dive into the heart of Florentine cuisine at Trattoria Mario. This unassuming eatery, tucked away from the tourist paths, serves up authentic pasta dishes. Try the ribollita soup or a classic plate of pappardelle al ragù.

Afternoon: 1:30 PM - 5:00 PM

Ponte Vecchio:
Cross the Ponte Vecchio, Florence's oldest bridge, lined with vibrant shops. Capture the charm of the Arno River and perhaps pick up a souvenir or two from the jewellers that dot the bridge.

Boboli Gardens:
Retreat to the Boboli Gardens behind the Pitti Palace for a leisurely stroll. The meticulously landscaped gardens offer a serene escape, providing a perfect backdrop for photos or a quiet moment of reflection.

Evening: 5:00 PM - 8:00 PM

Gelato at Vivoli:

Treat your taste buds to a scoop of heaven at Vivoli, one of Florence's oldest gelato shops. Choose from a myriad of flavors crafted with traditional methods that have stood the test of time.

Piazza della Signoria:
  End your day at Piazza della Signoria, the political heart of Florence. Admire the sculptures in the open-air museum, including a replica of Michelangelo's David. As the sun sets, soak in the vibrant atmosphere of this historical square.

Dinner: 8:00 PM Onward

Osteria Santo Spirito:
Conclude your day with a delightful dinner at Osteria Santo Spirito. Located in the Oltrarno district, this charming osteria offers a cozy ambiance and a menu brimming with Tuscan flavors. Indulge in local specialties like bistecca alla fiorentina or ribollita.

Nightcap: 10:00 PM - 11:00 PM

Piazzale Michelangelo: For a breathtaking night panorama of Florence, head to Piazzale Michelangelo. The city lights shimmer below, casting an enchanting glow on the Arno River. It's the perfect way to bid farewell to this captivating city.

• Weekend Getaway

Day 1: Morning - Immerse in Renaissance Art

Begin your day by seeing the world-famous Uffizi Gallery, which is home to Michelangelo, Leonardo da Vinci, and Botticelli masterpieces. Admire "Primavera" and "The Birth of Venus" with awe before crossing the famous Ponte Vecchio bridge.

Day 1: Florence's Culinary Delights in the Afternoon

Visit Mercato Centrale for a locally inspired lunch. Savour delicacies from Tuscany, such as pappa al pomodoro and ribollita. After that, stroll through Florence's streets, making stops at artisanal stores and Gelateria La Carraia for some sweets.

Day 1: Evening: Piazzale Michelangelo Sunset

Scale Piazzale Michelangelo for a stunning overview of Florence from above. The city comes to life as the sun sets, creating a breathtaking backdrop. Savour a special meal for two at a neighbourhood trattoria in the Oltrarno neighbourhood.

Day 2: Morning: Explore Florence's Cathedral

Start your day by visiting the Duomo, Florence's cathedral. Reach the summit of Giotto's Campanile for a breathtaking cityscape panorama. Examine the interior of the Baptistry and Cathedral while taking in the exquisite architecture and frescoes.

Day 2: Boboli Gardens and Artistic Enclaves in the Afternoon

Explore the equally lovely, but lesser-known, San Lorenzo neighbourhood. After touring the Medici Chapels, take a leisurely stroll around the Boboli Gardens. Take note of the amphitheatre, one of the gardens' hidden treasures.

Day 2: Dinner: A Real Florentine Experience

Osteria All'Antico Vinaio serves a typical Tuscan meal to round off your weekend. Savour a range of bruschettas and filling pasta meals while sipping on a regional Chianti. Finish off your evening with a scoop of Grom gelato.

CHAPTER ELEVEN

Conclusion

• Final Thoughts

It has been a captivating trip through history, art, and delicious food to explore Florence. Every step you take is reflected in the city's rich cultural tapestry, from the recognisable Duomo to the ageless masterpieces of the Uffizi Gallery. I leave with more than just memories as I bid adieu to the picturesque cobblestone streets and the tranquil reflections of the Arno River. I also bring with me a deep appreciation for Florence's enduring charm. I hope your journey through this Renaissance treasure is just as fascinating and unforgettable as mine was. Florence, till we cross paths again, ciao.

Printed in Great Britain
by Amazon